How to play

CRICKET

a step·by·step guide

Text:
Liz French

Technical consultant:
Derek Cousins
Secretary
Norfolk Cricket
Association

JARROLD

Other sports covered in this series are:

AMERICAN FOOTBALL   **SAILING A DINGHY**
BADMINTON   **SNOOKER**
BASKETBALL   **SOCCER**
BOWLS   **SQUASH**
COARSE FISHING   **SWIMMING**
CROQUET   **TABLE TENNIS**
GET FIT FOR SPORT   **TENNIS**
GOLF   **WINDSURFING**
HOCKEY

How to play CRICKET
ISBN 0-7117-0489-9

Text © Liz French 1991
This edition © Jarrold Publishing 1991
Illustrations by Ryz Hajdul

First published 1991
Reprinted 1994

Designed and produced by
Parke Sutton Limited, Norwich
for Jarrold Publishing, Norwich
Printed in Great Britain 2/94

Contents

Introduction

If you've caught the cricket bug, you're in excellent company! Cricket is one of the most universally popular games of all time, enjoyed by young and old alike and by both sexes. Its appeal is easy to understand. It offers a great combination of individual skill and team effort. It demands a variety of skills. And it is supremely enjoyable both to play and to watch.

It's not hard to get started in cricket, even if you haven't been in a team before. Almost every town and village has its own team and many will welcome enthusiastic newcomers. Your best starting point as a complete beginner is to find a club which has a coaching scheme (and a youth section if you are a junior). Ask around your friends and look in your local paper's sports pages for clues about local teams — or contact your library.

The 'Sports Clubs' listing in *Yellow Pages* are another good source of local information, or you can contact the National Cricket Association direct at Lord's Cricket Ground, London NW8 8QZ (tel: 0171 289 6098) and ask for the address and phone number of your nearest club.

This book is designed to give you a good understanding of the basics of the game and help you improve your batting, bowling and fielding skills. It also gives you some practical tips on anything from choosing a bat to keeping a scoresheet and some suggestions for practising on your own. You'll find the glossary at the back useful for looking up unfamiliar terms encountered in the book or while listening to commentators on television. Unfamiliar words are printed in italics and explained in the glossary on pages 47-48.

Of course, reading about the game is no substitute for actually playing it. This book won't turn you into a Test cricketer overnight — but it will help you get started and make the most of your game.

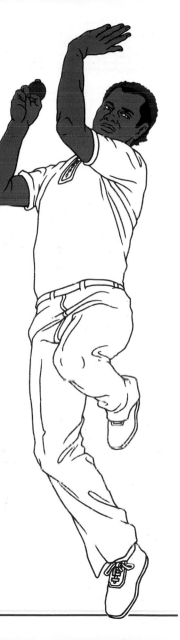

The Field

Cricket can be played on any size playing field with marked outer boundaries. Play centres on the pitch, a carefully mown and rolled flat area near the middle of the field.
Many grounds have more than one pitch kept ready, though changing pitches is not allowed once a match is in progress. Artificial pitches are sometimes found.
    The pitch must be of specified dimensions as shown here, although the distance between the wickets may be reduced for school or other games for young players.

Junior Game

Recommended guidelines for under-14 cricket:

- Pitch length
    (under-11) 18-19 yds (16.5-17.4 m)
    (under 12-13) 10-21 yds (18.3-19.2 m).

- Ball — 4¾oz weight (134.6 gms).

- Wickets and bats proportionately smaller.

- Under-13 must stand no nearer than 11 yds (10 m) from the bat in front of the wicket.

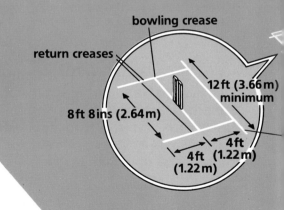

bowling crease

return creases

12 ft (3.66 m) minimum

8 ft 8 ins (2.64 m)

4 ft (1.22 m)

4 ft (1.22 m)

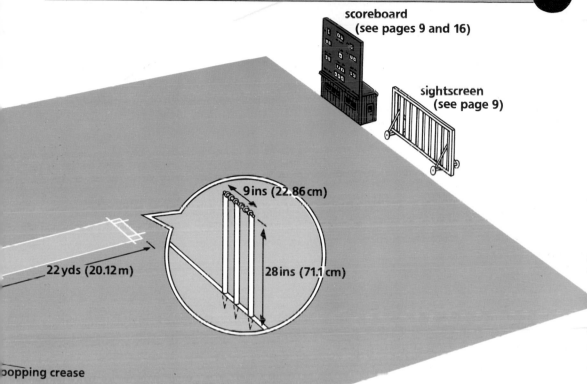

scoreboard
(see pages 9 and 16)

sightscreen
(see page 9)

9 ins (22.86 cm)

22 yds (20.12 m)

28 ins (71.1 cm)

popping crease

The creases

At each end of the pitch creases (lines) are drawn. These show:
● Where the bowler may place his feet when delivering a ball (see page 22).
● Where the batsman must stand while waiting for a delivery (see page 32).
● Where the batsman must reach after a run (see page 20).

The wickets

The wickets are positioned directly opposite each other at both ends of the pitch, 22 yds (20.12 m) apart. Each set consists of three equal-sized wooden stumps, and two wooden bails which fit into grooves cut in the domed tops of the stumps. Stumps have pointed ends to push into the ground.

Equipment

The bat

The bat must be made of wood and there are specified maximum lengths and widths as shown here. Subject to these limits, bats come in different weights and lengths of handle, and it is largely a matter of personal preference (see Hint box: choosing a bat, opposite).

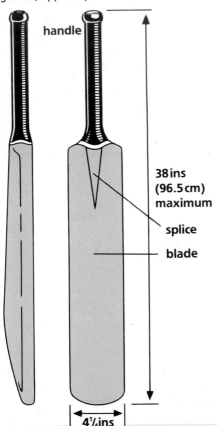

handle

38 ins
(96.5 cm)
maximum

splice

blade

4¼ins
(10.8 cm)

Hint box: choosing a bat

● Don't rush out as a complete beginner and buy a bat — you won't know the weight and length to suit you until you have some experience of playing the game.

● Go to a reputable specialist sports shop and take your time choosing.

● Try the 'feel' of many different bats — does the balance suit you?

● Can you lift it easily with one hand? If not, it's too heavy.

● Look down the length of the blade to make sure the grain is even and straight.

Care of your bat

● If it is pure willow, oil the face of your bat lightly with linseed oil before the cricket season starts — though many modern bats are pre-treated and will not need this.

● Avoid oiling the splice (the part where the handle joins the blade).

● Clean your bat regularly, using extra fine sandpaper when necessary.

● Break a new bat in by bouncing an old ball repeatedly on the blade.

The ball

Good quality cricket balls are made of cork tightly bound with twine inside a case of red leather. Cheaper balls made of plastic or other materials are OK for informal games and practice. A continuous seam is stitched around the middle of all cricket balls, which is an important aid for the bowler (see pages 24 and 29-31).

Dimensions and weights vary according to the level of game — this illustration shows a standard ball, though a smaller, lighter ball is often used for juniors.

weight: 5¹⁄₃ oz - 5³⁄₄ oz
(156-163 gm)
circumference: 8 ¹³⁄₁₆ ins - 9 ins
(22.4-22.9 cm)

Sightscreens

Two large, white sightscreens are sometimes positioned in the field, on the boundary fence behind each wicket.
These ensure that the receiving batsman has a clear view of the bowler's arm during delivery.

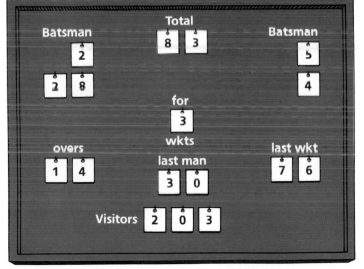

Scoreboard

Major cricket grounds have electronic scoreboards giving very detailed information about the state of play. Most smaller clubs have a basic scoreboard similar to the one shown here. See page 16 for what it all means!

Dress

Traditional cricket dress consists of all-white trousers for men and skirts for women, white shirt and white sweater.

Shoes

A pair of special white cricket shoes is a wise investment. Top-class players have different shoes for bowling, batting and fielding, but for a beginner one good pair of spike-soled canvas shoes with reinforced toecaps is fine.

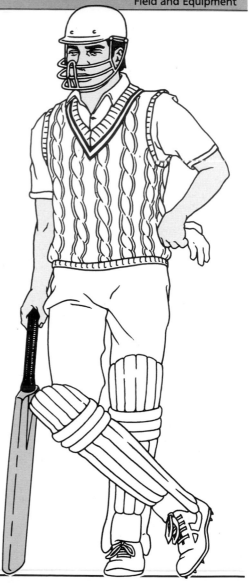

Hint box: buying shoes

- Go to a good sports shop.

- Choose spiked rather than rubber soles — they give better grip.

- Comfort is top priority — lace them up properly in the shop and walk around in them.

- Allow for wearing thick woollen socks.

Protective clothing

Cricket is a physical game and the ball is hard. Every batsman will take an occasional knock and some items of protective clothing are essential. Others are optional but can greatly improve your confidence in the face of fast bowling.

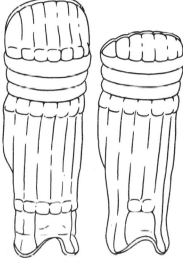

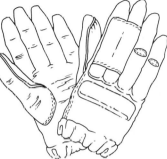

Leg pads

- Essential for wicketkeepers and batsmen.

- Wicketkeepers' pads are wider and sometimes shorter.

- Available in different sizes — make sure they fit comfortably.

- Buckle at the back with three straps.

Box

- Essential for male players.

Thigh pad, chest guard, elbow and arm pads

- Optional.

Protective helmet

- Optional — normally only used by batsmen and *close fielders* in top-class club cricket and above. However, wearing a helmet in any match against a dangerous bowler could be a good idea!

- Made of metal or fibreglass.

- Available in a variety of sizes and designs.

- Check for good close fit.

- Check for safety standards.

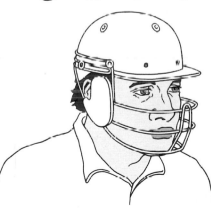

Batting gloves

- Essential for all batsmen.

- Leather palm gives good grip.

- Padded 'fingers' on the back.

Wicketkeeping gloves

- Made of leather.

- Built-in protection (sponge, rubber and cane).

The Players

Cricket is played between two sides, normally with eleven players each. The teams take it in turns to either bat (take their *innings*) or field. The fielding team has all its players on the field, but only two batsmen play at any one time, one at each end of the pitch. The aim of the game is, of course, to score more runs than your opponents.

In top-class cricket, players often develop specialist skills. Whilst some are outstanding bowlers, others excel at batting. As a beginner, you should try to develop a good all-round game. EVERY player should be competent at fielding.

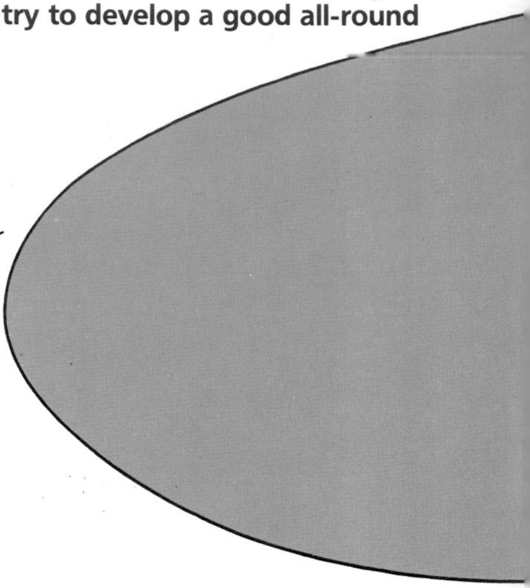

Batsmen (red in diagram)

Two batsmen are on the field at any one time in the match; the rest of the team wait in the pavilion (if there isn't one, sit outside the boundary!). A team often sends its two strongest batsmen in first (the 'openers'). Batsmen stand at opposite ends of the pitch, in their *creases*. They stay in the innings until given out (see pages 18-21).

Aims: ● To strike the ball and score as many runs as possible.

● To avoid being out.

Bowler (yellow in diagram)

Teams usually have four or more bowlers. A bowler chosen by the captain will take a turn to deliver the six balls that make up an *over* from one end of the pitch to the batsman receiving at the other. When six balls have been bowled, another bowler delivers the next six from the other end. No bowler may deliver consecutive overs in a match.

Aims: ● To get the batsman out.

● To prevent the batsman making a scoring stroke.

Fielders (blue in diagram)

Apart from the bowler, all the other players in the non-batting team take up various positions around the field. This diagram shows typical positions for fielding against a right-handed batsman, but there are many other possible positions (see page 39). Wicketkeeping is a specialist fielding role and is considered on page 44.

Aims: ● To retrieve the ball as quickly as possible.

● To prevent runs being scored.

● To get the batsman out.

Umpires (white on diagram)
(see next page)

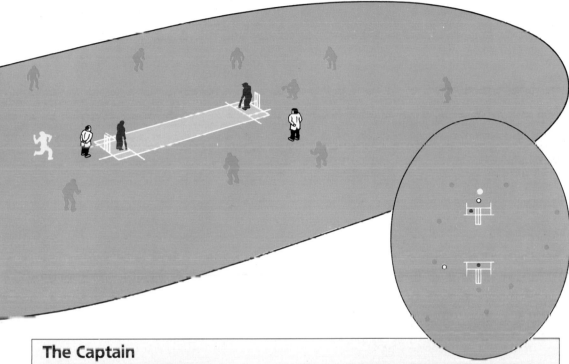

The Captain

One of the players in each team is also the captain. This is a responsible position and the team looks to its captain for guidance and inspiration. The captain's job is to:

- Lead and motivate the team by example and positive attitude.
- Decide batting order. • Decide who bowls and when. • Decide fielding positions.
- Make sure the team is kept informed on fielding, bowling and batting tactics.
- Take the toss at the start of the match and, if winning it decides whether to bat or field first.
- Decide when to *declare*.

The Umpires

The game is controlled by two umpires, positioned as shown on page 13, one by the bowler's wicket and the other on the leg side of the batsman's wicket. Umpires wear white coats and use a number of different signals to indicate decisions.

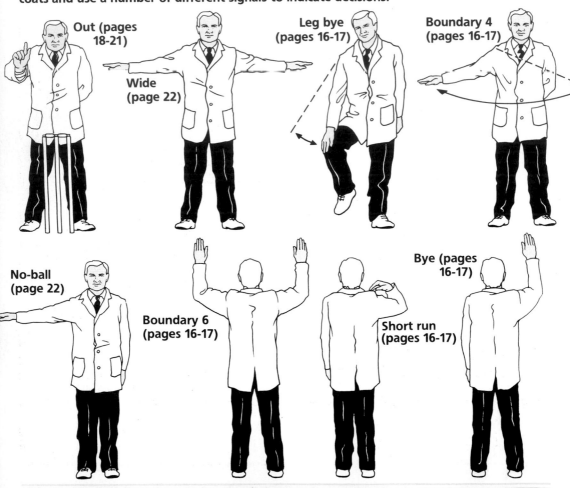

Out (pages 18-21)

Wide (page 22)

Leg bye (pages 16-17)

Boundary 4 (pages 16-17)

No-ball (page 22)

Boundary 6 (pages 16-17)

Short run (pages 16-17)

Bye (pages 16-17)

The Game

Starting

The game begins with one of the captains (usually the home captain) tossing a coin, the winner deciding whether to bat or field first.

- The fielding side comes onto the field first.

- The opening batsmen then take up position.

- When the umpires are also in place, the bowler delivers the first ball.

An over

An over consists of six deliveries from the bowler from one end of the pitch. *Wides* and *no-balls* don't count as part of the over. The umpire keeps track of the number of balls bowled, and after six fair deliveries calls 'over' and the bowler and fielders change ends. The batsmen stay where they are. No bowler may bowl consecutive overs in one innings.

Duration

A match can vary in duration.

- A school game will often be played in one afternoon, with each team having either a certain number of overs, or a time limit on their innings.

- County Championship matches last four days.

- Test matches last five days, with a minimum of 90 overs a day.

- Limited-over (one-day) matches are also common in top level cricket.

An innings

An innings is the period of play in which a team takes its turn at batting; it lasts until ten batsmen are out, the agreed number of *overs* have been bowled, the agreed time limit reached, or the innings is *declared.* A match can be of one or two innings of each side. In a two-innings match, the teams take it in turns to take their innings except when the follow-on rule is applied.

Follow-on rule

Once both teams have taken their first innings, the team batting second can be asked to bat again if they are losing by more than a certain margin, which varies according to the length of the match.

Scoring

A run

The score is reckoned in runs, which are gained in a number of ways.

Boundary

If you hit the ball across the boundary of the field, there is no need actually to run to score (though you should always run unless you are **completely** sure the ball will reach the boundary). A boundary is worth **four** runs if it crosses the boundary after having bounced in the field of play, or **six** if it crosses over before touching the ground.

Ones, twos, threes

To score runs from a stroke which doesn't reach the boundary, you and the other batsman run between the wickets from one popping crease to the other as many times as you dare before the fielders can knock down one or other of the wickets with the ball. You must both ground your bats beyond the opposite *popping crease* for each run (if you don't the run is termed a *short run* and doesn't count). You might occasionally get four runs this way though a field would have to be very big for the ball to take that long to reach the boundary!

A scoreboard

Here's the basic scoreboard shown on page 9, with the numbers explained.

The home team have scored 83 runs for 3 wickets (that is, three batsmen have been given out).

Batsman No. 2 has scored 28 runs, No. 5 has scored 4. The last man scored 30 runs and the last wicket fell at 76. This innings is in its 14th over and the other side scored 203 in their innings.

Extras

You can also score without even touching the ball with your bat. Runs acquired this way are termed *extras* and come from byes, leg byes, wides or no-balls.

● A *bye* is scored when the ball passes the wicket untouched by bat or batsman and the batsmen successfully run between the wickets.

● A *leg bye* is scored when the batsman unintentionally touches the ball with any part of the body or equipment other than the bat or hand holding it and successfully completes a run.

● One run is added to the team's score (but not the batsman's individual score) if the umpire calls a *no-ball* or a *wide*. You can't be bowled, stumped, *lbw* or caught after a no-ball or a wide. But if the ball travels some distance, you may decide to run anyway, in which case you can be run out in the usual way.

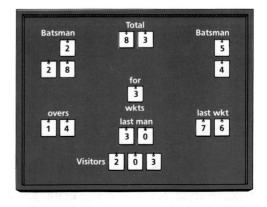

Score-keeping and Analysis

If you like playing around with figures, cricket scores can give endless fun. As well as keeping running totals and detailed information about a match in progress, you may also like to analyse a team or individual performance during and at the end of a season.

Here's a typical scoresheet.

BATSMEN	RUNS SCORED	HOW OUT	BOWLER	TOTAL
1 T THOMPSON	1./.1./.1.1.2./.1.4../.1.2./.1.2./.1.2.1./.1.2.1./.1.	RUN OUT		34
2 G HARRIS	2.4.2.4.1./.1.4./.	BOWLED	I McINNES	20
3 H MATTHEWS	1.2.2.4.1. /	CT LAKE	G SMITH	10
4 B JONES	1.1.	BOWLED	G SMITH	2
5 L WOODS	1.1.2.1.1.	L B W	P LYONS	6
6 S READ	1.1.	NOT OUT		2
7 J BURGESS				
8 A JARROLD				

HARRINGTON CRICKET CLUB V WESTMINSTER C. CLUB
HOME CLUB INNINGS OF WESTMINSTER PLAYED AT BORHAM GREEN ON 30TH JULY 19 91

TOTAL AT THE FALL OF EACH WICKET AND NO. OF OUTGOING BATSMAN										
1 FOR	2 FOR	3 FOR	4 FOR	5 FOR	6 FOR	7 FOR	8 FOR	9 FOR	10 FOR	
36	49	59	78	88						
2	3	4	1	5						

BYES	1.4.1.4.	EXTRAS	12
LEG BYES	1.	TOTAL	88
WIDES	1.	FOR 5 WKTS.	
NO BALLS			

Typical bowling analysis

SCORER W. DUNCOMBE BOWLING ANALYSIS. HARRINGTON CLUB

BOWLERS	1-20 (over-by-over)	NO BALLS	WIDES	BALLS BOWLED	OVERS	MDN OVERS	RUNS	WKTS	AVGE
1 B COLLINS				13	2	–	5	–	–
2 W DEAN				30	5	1	18	–	–
3 I McINNES				30	5	1	20	1	20·00
4 G SMITH				30	5	–	18	2	9·00
5 P LYONS				18	3	–	15	1	15·00
			1	121	20	2	76	4	19·00

START 2.30 PM FINISH 7.00 PM RESULT HARRINGTON WON UMPIRES ASHWORTH & ROMAN

M: Maiden CT: Caught

For each over, the six dots represent the six deliveries, and runs scored are written in over the appropriate dot. You can fill in the totals at the end of the match.

PLAYING: SOME RULES

This book is not intended to give you a comprehensive explanation of all the laws of cricket, which are many and complex and designed to cover every possible event. You do, however, need a clear understanding of the basics: what you can and cannot do when batting, fielding and bowling.

Batting: Howzat?

You can be 'out' for any of a variety of reasons — but only if a member of the fielding side appeals to the umpire before the next ball is delivered. The appeal must be in the form of 'How's that?'. If you are obviously and fairly out, though, you should walk to the pavilion without waiting for an appeal.

1 Caught

You are caught out if a fielder catches the ball before it touches the ground after it has touched your bat (or the hand, glove or below the wrist that is holding the bat).

2 Handled the ball

You will be out if you touch the ball on purpose with the hand not on the bat, unless the other team consent to your touching it.

3 Timed out

When you are coming on to replace a batsman who's been dismissed, you are allowed two minutes to step onto the field — take longer and you'll be given out.

4 Bowled

You are bowled out if the bowler knocks one or both bails off your wicket (the wicket is said to be 'down' or 'broken'). To be bowled, the ball must touch the wicket direct from the bowler's delivery or be played onto the wicket by the bat or any part of your person. If the ball touches the stump and the bails wobble but don't fall, breathe a sigh of relief — you are not out.

5 Hit the ball twice

Once you have hit the ball, or it has hit any part of you, you'll be out if you deliberately try to strike it again. An exception is made if the second strike is made solely to stop the ball hitting the wicket — but in this case no runs can be scored except for *overthrows*.

6 Hit wicket

You'll be out 'hit wicket' if you knock the bails off yourself while preparing for or making a shot, or starting off on your first run. If you break the wicket in the normal course of running, or while avoiding a run out, you won't be out.

7 Obstructing the field

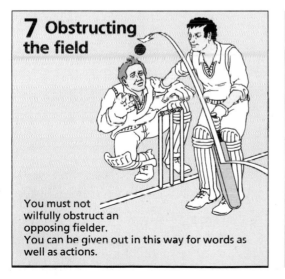

You must not wilfully obstruct an opposing fielder.
You can be given out in this way for words as well as actions.

8 Stumped

If you are completely outside the popping crease because of making a stroke, and the wicket is knocked down with the ball by the wicketkeeper, you are out 'stumped'. If you have already started running you are not stumped but 'run out' (see page 20).

9 Run out

When running between wickets, you must touch the ground with your bat ('ground' it) in the opposite *popping crease* before a fielder puts down the wicket. If you need to, you can make a dive for it, but the bat must still be in your hand. If a fielder puts down the wicket **before** you make good your ground, you are run out.

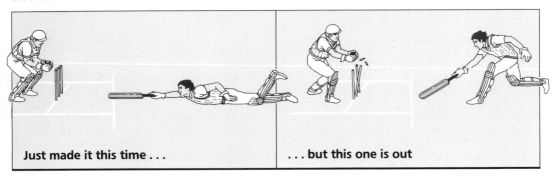

Just made it this time . . .   . . . but this one is out

Run out — which batsman?

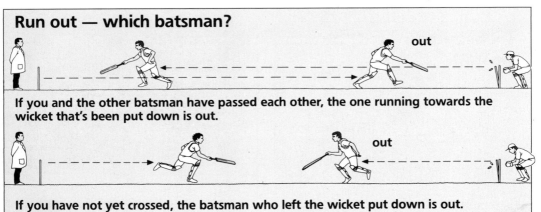

If you and the other batsman have passed each other, the one running towards the wicket that's been put down is out.

If you have not yet crossed, the batsman who left the wicket put down is out.

If one batsman has not left his ground, or returns to it, and the other batsman joins him there, the latter is out.

10 Leg before wicket (lbw)

This method of being dismissed often causes confusion and is dependent on the umpire's opinion.

The point of the lbw rule is to stop batsmen from blocking the wicket with anything other than the bat. You must not intercept a fair ball, which would otherwise have hit the wicket, with any part of your body or equipment (except to hit it with your bat, of course — or the hand holding the bat).

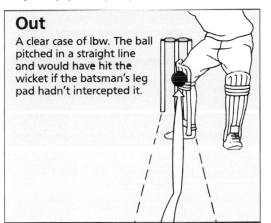

Out

A clear case of lbw. The ball pitched in a straight line and would have hit the wicket if the batsman's leg pad hadn't intercepted it.

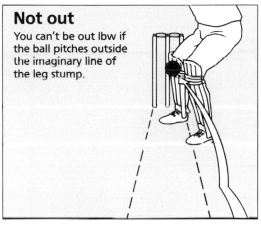

Not out

You can't be out lbw if the ball pitches outside the imaginary line of the leg stump.

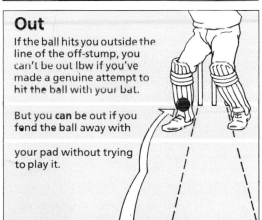

Out

If the ball hits you outside the line of the off-stump, you can't be out lbw if you've made a genuine attempt to hit the ball with your bat.

But you **can** be out if you fend the ball away with

your pad without trying to play it.

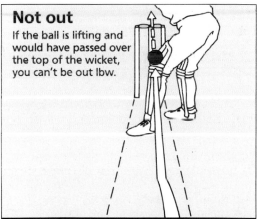

Not out

If the ball is lifting and would have passed over the top of the wicket, you can't be out lbw.

Note: dotted lines indicate imaginary lines drawn straight down the pitch from stump to stump.

Bowling: No-Balls

When bowling, there are certain requirements for a lawful delivery. Any infringements of these conditions result in a *no-ball* being called.

● A batsman can still score runs off a no-ball and can be run out, but not bowled, caught, lbw or stumped.

● If the batsman does not make any runs off a no-ball, one run is automatically added to the batting team's score (but not to the batsman's individual score); runs scored in this way are termed *extras* (see pages 16-17).

● Whether or not any runs are made, another delivery is added at the end of the over to replace the no-ball.

---

1 You must tell the umpire, who in turn tells the batsman, whether you are intending to bowl overarm or underarm (underarm is very rarely used), which side of the wicket you will bowl, and whether you will bowl right or left-handed.

2 You must bowl, not throw the ball — i.e. you mustn't straighten your bowling arm immediately before the ball leaves your hand.

---

3 Your back foot must be inside the return crease, not touching it. Your front foot must not be beyond the popping crease.

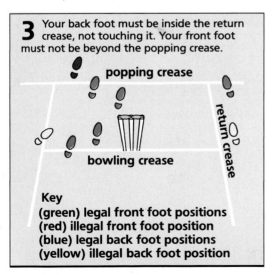

Key
(green) legal front foot positions
(red) illegal front foot position
(blue) legal back foot positions
(yellow) illegal back foot position

4 Wide ball

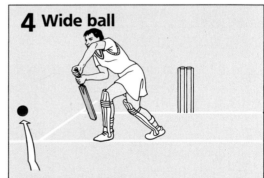

A ball is deemed wide if it is too high or wide for the striker to play when taking his or her normal guard. Like a no-ball, one run is automatically added to the team score if no runs result, and a replacement delivery added at the end of the over.

Fielding Positions: No-Balls

You will see from the fielding technique section (page 39) that a fielding team has a wide choice of field placings. There are, however, some restrictions, and the umpire will call a *no-ball* if these are contravened.

1 The wicketkeeper must stay completely behind the wicket until the ball has touched the bat or batsman, or passed the wicket, or until the batsman attempts a run.

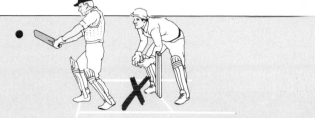

2 There must not be more than two *on-side* fielders behind the *popping crease* as the bowler delivers the ball.

3 While the ball is in play, and until it is struck by, or has passed the batsman, no fielder other than the bowler may stand on the pitch.

BOWLING

Note: For convenience, instructions given throughout this and subsequent sections apply to right-handed players; apologies to left-handers, who should simply reverse the appropriate references.

The Basics

Bowling is one of the most fascinating and challenging aspects of the game. Developing good bowling skills takes practice but the satisfaction of forcing a batsman into making a mistake makes the effort well worthwhile! Although bowling should be one smooth action, it can be broken down into four basic elements — grip, run-up, delivery and follow-through.

Grip

How you hold the ball depends on the type of delivery, and you'll find some variations covered in the following pages. But you should concentrate on mastering this basic grip first. The most important point to note is that you grip with your fingers, not your palms.

1 Put your first two fingers on either side of the seam, and your thumb directly underneath and touching the seam.

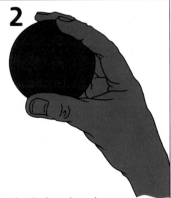

2 Check that there is a gap between your palm and the 'V' made by your thumb and first finger.

Run-up

Rhythm is the key word in the run-up to the wicket. Once you've got it right, your run-up should always be the same, so practise until it is so consistent that you could do it blindfolded.

The run-up should contain an odd number of paces — say five, seven, nine or eleven — but can vary in length according to your style of bowling; usually the longer the run-up, the faster the delivery. As a general rule, keep your run-up as short as you can.

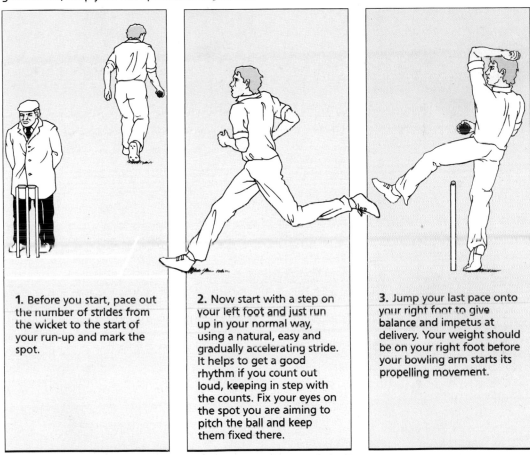

1. Before you start, pace out the number of strides from the wicket to the start of your run-up and mark the spot.

2. Now start with a step on your left foot and just run up in your normal way, using a natural, easy and gradually accelerating stride. It helps to get a good rhythm if you count out loud, keeping in step with the counts. Fix your eyes on the spot you are aiming to pitch the ball and keep them fixed there.

3. Jump your last pace onto your right foot to give balance and impetus at delivery. Your weight should be on your right foot before your bowling arm starts its propelling movement.

Delivery

The delivery should be a smooth continuation of the run-up: otherwise you'll lose your rhythm and momentum. The easier and more fluent the action, the more accurate the delivery.

● As you reach the wicket, your left shoulder points towards the batsman and your left hand is high above your head.

● Weight is still on the back foot.

● The bowling hand is held under your chin.

● Keep your eyes on the target.

● Lean your body slightly away from the batsman.

● As your weight is transferred onto your front foot your body is thrown into the delivery and the ball is released naturally.

● Hips and shoulders have turned naturally to face the opposite wicket.

● Back leg is off the ground ready for follow-through.

Follow-through

A good follow-through is essential to successful bowling and will vary in distance according to the pace of your delivery. It's really a question of natural momentum taking you on a few steps, but there are some principles to observe.

1. The first stride is towards the batsman. Your right knee leads and your eyes should still be looking at the spot you are aiming to pitch the ball. Your bowling arm follows through on its action, too, cutting across your body, while the left arm goes well back.

2. As you slow down, move to the left and away from the pitch so as not to cause it any damage. In fact it is an offence to damage the pitch, so be careful.

Length

As a beginner, accuracy is more important than pace. Practise until you can consistently deliver accurate balls to a good length. Being able to vary your length to take the batsman by surprise is also very useful. But what exactly **is** a 'good length' delivery?

A good length can be described as a delivery which pitches at the point which causes the batsman most confusion. If the batsman has to hesitate over whether to play back or forward, that's a good length delivery. The perfect length will vary depending on a number of factors: the pace of the ball, for example, or the state of the pitch; even the age and condition of the ball.

Balls which fall short or long are known by different names and these are shown here.

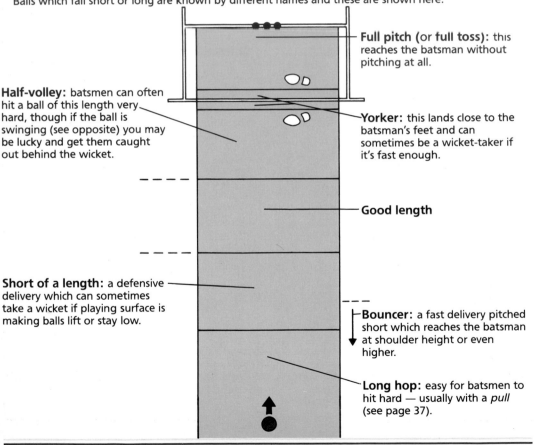

Full pitch (or full toss): this reaches the batsman without pitching at all.

Half-volley: batsmen can often hit a ball of this length very hard, though if the ball is swinging (see opposite) you may be lucky and get them caught out behind the wicket.

Yorker: this lands close to the batsman's feet and can sometimes be a wicket-taker if it's fast enough.

Good length

Short of a length: a defensive delivery which can sometimes take a wicket if playing surface is making balls lift or stay low.

Bouncer: a fast delivery pitched short which reaches the batsman at shoulder height or even higher.

Long hop: easy for batsmen to hit hard — usually with a *pull* (see page 37).

Swing-Bowling

This is a style of bowling where the ball is made to take a curved path in flight. By varying the direction the seam on the ball is facing, and the amount of shine on the ball, you can influence its flight curve. The amount of deviation (*break*) from a straight path will be affected by wind and air pressure.

Tip: ever wondered why bowlers often rub the ball on their trousers? It's because a shiny ball helps the ball to swing.

In-swinger

The in-swinger curves away to the leg side.

Preparation and grip

Polish only half the ball as shown; grip with seam facing towards fine leg, fingertips either side of the seam on top and thumb flat against the seam underneath.

Delivery

Have your bowling arm very high at delivery; aim at the off-stump to allow for curve in flight.

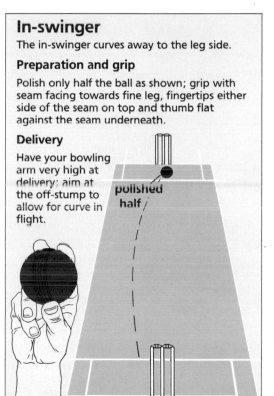

Out-swinger

This is the opposite to an in-swinger, curving to the off side.

Preparation and grip

Polish only half the ball as shown; grip is similar to the basic grip (see page 24) but aim the seam towards the first slip.

Delivery

At the moment of release, your wrist should be held firm, fingers behind the ball.

Spin-Bowling

Off-spin

An off-spinner is a relatively slow bowler who tries to make the ball deviate from the off towards the leg after pitching. Because of the slower speed, a successful off-spinner needs to be a master of bowling a length. Too short and the batsman has plenty of time to determine the angle of the off break; over-pitched and he can step out and hit the ball on the full toss without giving it a chance to turn.

Preparation and grip

Place your first and second fingers across the seam with your thumb lying naturally along the seam and the other two fingers supporting the ball underneath.

Delivery

As the ball is bowled, cock your wrist back. The spin is imparted by your first finger which drops sharply downwards with your thumb flipping upwards. Immediately after the ball is bowled, your hand cuts across your body, finishing with palm pointing upwards.

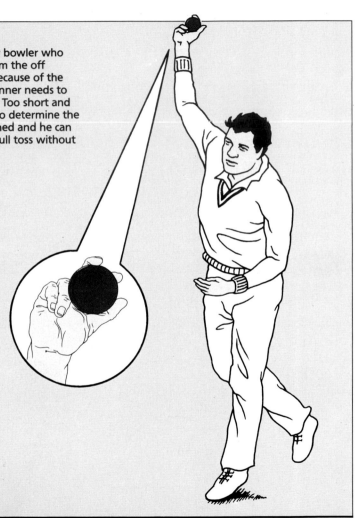

Leg-spin

Though often faster than an off-spinner, a leg-spinner is also a slow bowler. This time the idea is to make the ball *break* the opposite way, from the leg towards the off. It is an attacking style of bowling which can take a lot of wickets — but many batsmen also find it easier to score runs from leg-spin than from off-spin.

Preparation and grip

Grip the ball with your first two fingers and the top joint of your thumb, at a natural distance apart, across the seam. Your third finger — which does all the work — should be bent so that its side lies along the seam.

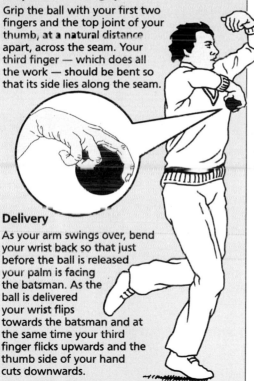

Delivery

As your arm swings over, bend your wrist back so that just before the ball is released your palm is facing the batsman. As the ball is delivered your wrist flips towards the batsman and at the same time your third finger flicks upwards and the thumb side of your hand cuts downwards.

Googly

This is a development of the leg-spin and results in an off-break. It can surprise even the best batsmen if they are not watching the bowler's hand. Exciting though it is, you shouldn't attempt to bowl the googly until you are proficient at leg-spinning.

Preparation and grip

As for leg-spin.

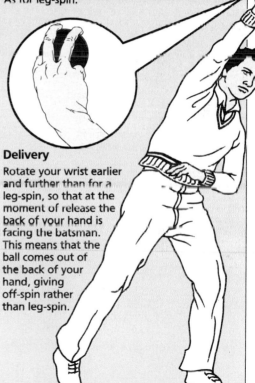

Delivery

Rotate your wrist earlier and further than for a leg-spin, so that at the moment of release the back of your hand is facing the batsman. This means that the ball comes out of the back of your hand, giving off-spin rather than leg-spin.

The Basics

You can learn best by watching good players in action and from constant practice. This section will help you master the basics of successful batting. But there are no rigid rules and you should never be afraid of hitting the ball in a natural and uninhibited way.

Grip

You need to grip the bat firmly — but not tightly — with both hands, not just the bottom hand. The best way is to pick the bat up without thinking too much about it.

1. Put the bat on the ground in front of you and stand up straight with palms facing the ground and fingers pointing ahead.

2. Now just bend down and put both hands on the handle, close together and quite near the top.

3. Then check: are your fingers and thumbs wrapped well around?

 Can you see two 'V' shapes made by your thumbs and first fingers? — they should be in line with each other.

Taking guard

When you start batting, or change ends for the first time, you'll need to ask the umpire (or a friend if it's an informal game) to give you a *guard* so that you know exactly where the wickets are in relation to your bat without looking.

Hold the bat upright with its face towards the umpire. Ask for your preferred guard (middle, middle-and-leg or leg stump) and the umpire will direct your bat to the right position. Then make a mark (*block*) so that you can remember it whenever you face the bowler.

> ### Which guard?
>
> **The best guard is the one which naturally positions your head in line with the middle stump with your eyes level.**
>
>
>
> ● **If you have an upright stance, you'll probably want middle or middle-and-leg.**
>
> ● **If you tend to stoop, try a leg stump guard.**

A good grip allows you to move both wrists together and complete your follow-through properly.

Tip: the back of your left hand should always face the ball.

Stance

This may look complicated but the most important thing is to be comfortable and relaxed. From this position you can move quickly in any direction.

- Head up, facing down the wicket with eyes level.

- Left shoulder points towards bowler.

- Feet are up to 6 ins (15 cm) apart, either side of the *popping crease*.

- Weight evenly distributed.

- Knees slightly bent.

- Bat faces down the wicket and is grounded just behind the toe of the back foot.

- Top hand rests lightly on the pad of your left leg.

Backlift

This is the first movement of any batting stroke — raising the bat in preparation for your stroke. It should be a smooth, fluid movement.

- Start the backlift in good time so you don't have to rush the stroke.

- Bring the bat straight back and let your wrists cock naturally.

- Note that at the top of the backlift the left forearm should be parallel with the ground or even higher.

- The bat is straight above the stumps and your elbows are clear of your body.

- Keep your head still.

The Strokes

Different bowling styles need different kinds of stroke. Being a good batsman means being able to read or anticipate a delivery and make an instant decision on how to play it. With experience this will become almost second nature. Strokes can be made with either the front foot stepping down the wicket or with both feet behind the popping crease.

Defensive strokes

As a beginner your main objective is to stay in, so don't try to score runs off every delivery. These are the strokes for playing safe — practise them often.

Remember: ● Watch the ball.   ● Keep your bat as upright as possible.   ● Keep your top hand in front at impact so that the ball is hit downwards, not up in the air for an easy catch.

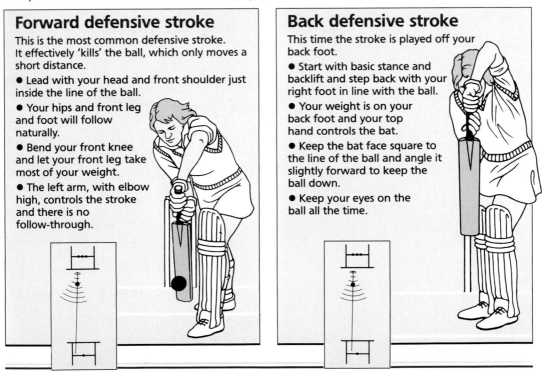

Forward defensive stroke

This is the most common defensive stroke. It effectively 'kills' the ball, which only moves a short distance.

● Lead with your head and front shoulder just inside the line of the ball.

● Your hips and front leg and foot will follow naturally.

● Bend your front knee and let your front leg take most of your weight.

● The left arm, with elbow high, controls the stroke and there is no follow-through.

Back defensive stroke

This time the stroke is played off your back foot.

● Start with basic stance and backlift and step back with your right foot in line with the ball.

● Your weight is on your back foot and your top hand controls the bat.

● Keep the bat face square to the line of the ball and angle it slightly forward to keep the ball down.

● Keep your eyes on the ball all the time.

The Drive

It's often said that a batsman who can't drive is only half a batsman. Not only is this a most satisfying stroke to make, but if you can't play it the bowler will soon find out and you'll find it very hard to make runs without getting out.

- The drive is most effective against an over-pitched ball that you can hit just as it comes off the ground
- The initial movement is the same as for a forward defensive stroke — so very often you can change from defence to attack without having to change the stroke completely.

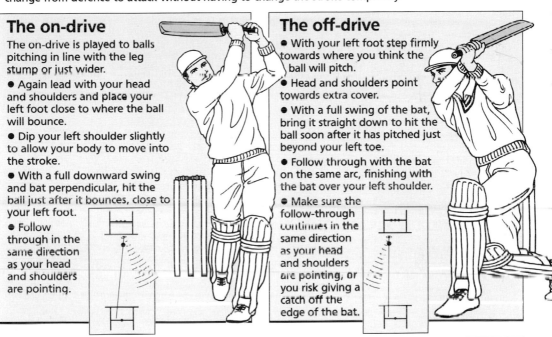

The on-drive

The on-drive is played to balls pitching in line with the leg stump or just wider.

- Again lead with your head and shoulders and place your left foot close to where the ball will bounce.
- Dip your left shoulder slightly to allow your body to move into the stroke.
- With a full downward swing and bat perpendicular, hit the ball just after it bounces, close to your left foot.
- Follow through in the same direction as your head and shoulders are pointing.

The off-drive

- With your left foot step firmly towards where you think the ball will pitch.
- Head and shoulders point towards extra cover.
- With a full swing of the bat, bring it straight down to hit the ball soon after it has pitched just beyond your left toe.
- Follow through with the bat on the same arc, finishing with the bat over your left shoulder.
- Make sure the follow-through continues in the same direction as your head and shoulders are pointing, or you risk giving a catch off the edge of the bat.

Moving out to drive

You can drive a good length ball from a slow bowler by stepping down the wicket and hitting the ball on the half-volley — but you'll need quick, neat footwork and an accurate estimate of where the ball will bounce. Even a slight miscalculation and you may miss the ball completely. If this happens, even if you are not bowled, you give the wicketkeeper a great chance to stump you.

On the Leg Side

Attacking strokes on the leg side — pulls and hooks — are great when you can make them, but a good bowler won't give you many chances. Over-frequent use of these strokes has been the downfall of many a young batsman — so only attempt one against a short ball pitched on, or just outside, the line of the stumps.

The difference between a *hook* and a *pull* is that the first is made only to fast balls that have bounced at least chest high, while the pull is made to slow and fast deliveries. Both shots are played off the back foot.

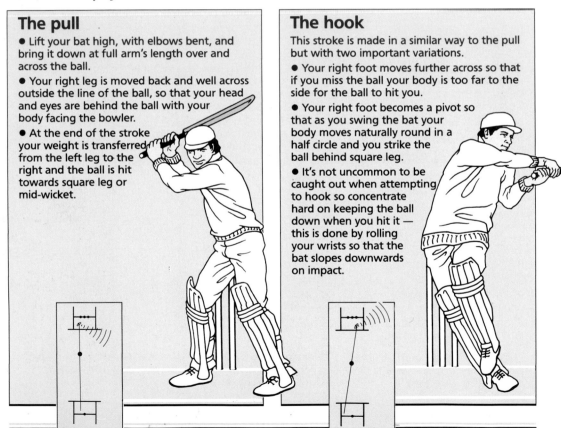

The pull

● Lift your bat high, with elbows bent, and bring it down at full arm's length over and across the ball.

● Your right leg is moved back and well across outside the line of the ball, so that your head and eyes are behind the ball with your body facing the bowler.

● At the end of the stroke your weight is transferred from the left leg to the right and the ball is hit towards square leg or mid-wicket.

The hook

This stroke is made in a similar way to the pull but with two important variations.

● Your right foot moves further across so that if you miss the ball your body is too far to the side for the ball to hit you.

● Your right foot becomes a pivot so that as you swing the bat your body moves naturally round in a half circle and you strike the ball behind square leg.

● It's not uncommon to be caught out when attempting to hook so concentrate hard on keeping the ball down when you hit it — this is done by rolling your wrists so that the bat slopes downwards on impact.

Behind the Wicket

You can score runs from deflections as well as hits, and the *cut* and *glance* are important strokes in any batsman's repertoire. They are not easy strokes, though, and you'll need lots of practice in the nets (see pages 46-47) before trying them out on the field.

The square cut

This stroke is nearly always made off the back foot and is safest against a short ball which is well wide of the off-stump. The stroke is directed to the left of point or else down the gulley.

● Throw your right foot across and bring the bat down hard, over and across the ball.

● Keep your weight firmly on your back foot.

● Flex your right knee slightly to help your balance.

● Keep your eye on the ball all the time.

The leg glance

This is best played to a ball pitched just short of a length on or outside the leg stump.

● Move your right foot back and across in front of the stumps with your right toe pointing down the pitch.

● As your body swivels round to make the stroke your right foot acts as a pivot.

● Contact is made with the ball just a few inches in front of your left leg.

● Left hand controls the bat until the last moment, when the right hand turns the face of the bat to deflect the ball down to long leg.

Taking Runs

Once you've made a stroke — assuming it's not obviously going to be a boundary — you have to decide whether or not to run.

To run or not to run?

- If you are going to run, you must let the other batsman know by calling 'yes'.
- If not, call 'no' or 'wait'.
- Once you have made a call, be positive: changing your mind or dithering can get you or the other batsman out.

Who decides?

- The striker calls 'yes' (or 'no') if the ball goes in front of the wicket.
- The non-striker should call if the ball has gone behind the wicket.

Hint box: striking batsman

- Don't settle for defensive play — go for scoring strokes when you can.
- Timing is probably the most important factor in successful batting — work on it.
- Always keep your eyes fixed on the ball.
- Keep a mental picture of where the fielders are so you can avoid hitting the ball directly to them.

Grounding the bat

Whether you're the striker or not, it's important to get your bat safely grounded at the end of a run as quickly as possible to avoid being run out. Ground it at least 2 yds (1.8 m) before the crease and run with it at arm's length along the ground — you'll get there more quickly and safely.

Hint box: non-striking batsman

- Stand just inside the *popping crease*, not next to the *bowling crease* — it will cut your running distance by a yard.
- Start walking forward as the bowler releases the ball and be ready to run if the batsman plays a scoring shot.
- Be ready to regain your ground instantly if the batsman hits a hard drive straight back towards the bowler.
- When running, be careful not to bump into the batsman! Avoid this by always running down the side of the pitch opposite to that on which the bowler is bowling.

Fielding Positions

There are many possible fielding positions, most shown on the diagram below. The exact positions adopted by a team will vary — according to the style of the bowler, the known strengths and weaknesses of the opponents and the instructions of the team's captain. The wicketkeeper's role is a specialist one, considered separately on pages 44 and 45.

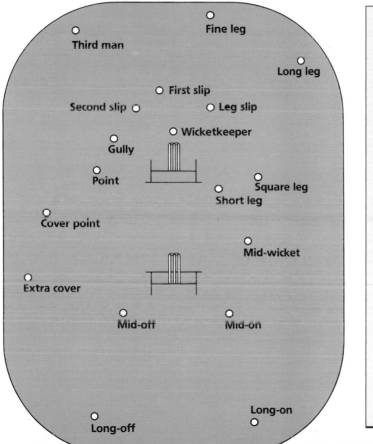

Variations on many of these can be used and these are defined by adding an extra word:
● 'Short . . .' means closer to the batsman.
● 'Long . . .' means further away.
● 'Silly . . .' is often used to describe mid-on, mid-off or point when positioned very close to the batsman.
● 'Backward . . .' and 'forward . . .' are used to position those fielders who are square with the wicket (point and square leg) either just behind the batsman or just in front of him.

Fielding Skills

Good fielding is essential to a team's success and ALL team members should be agile and competent retrievers, catchers and throwers.

Retrieving

Your main aim, of course, is to get to the ball and return it to the wicket — fast! This means that even if you are chasing a ball with your back to the wicket, you must have a picture in your mind of your exact position, so that once you have the ball you can turn and throw without delay.

1. Two-handed interception

Here the player safely intercepts the ball with both hands and then moves into position for throwing.

- If possible, move into the line of the ball by moving right (right-handed players).
- Have your right foot at right-angles to the ball as you drop to your left knee.
- Keep hands close together, fingers pointing down and touching the ground.
- Watch the ball until it's safely in your hands.
- Take one step, spinning round on your right foot to get into position to throw.

2. One-handed interception

Go for a two-handed retrieval when you can, but if speed is the main requirement one hand may have to do.

- Let your back foot trail to give balance when you're picking up the ball.
- Turn directly from the pick-up if you can, though sometimes your momentum will take you on a pace or two.

Throwing

Accuracy is all-important so practise throwing from different positions in the field. Speed is also vital, but not at the expense of accuracy. There should always be back-up from another player to stop overthrows at either wicket.

- For distance and accuracy use a long, rising overarm throw.
- For speed from the infield, throw from shoulder level.
- Non-throwing arm points at the target.

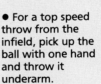

- For a top speed throw from the infield, pick up the ball with one hand and throw it underarm.
- Keep your eyes on your target.

Catching

Another vital skill for a good fielder. Making a spectacular catch is one of the most satisfying parts of the game — and can win the match.

● Cup your hands together slightly, nicely relaxed, palms facing the ball.
● Keep your eyes fixed on the ball until you are holding it safely. ● Keep your head as still as possible.

High catching

If you are at, or near, the boundary and the ball's flying through the air in your direction, don't panic!

● Stay relaxed and don't move until you can read the flight of the ball.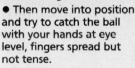

● Then move into position and try to catch the ball with your hands at eye level, fingers spread but not tense.

● Remember to keep your eyes on the ball all the time.

● Let your fingers 'give' with the ball as you catch it so that it's finally held close to your chest.

Close catching

Close fielding positions give you an opportunity for some really satisfying catching — so make sure you don't miss!
Again, practice is the answer.

● Get into a crouching position, feet comfortably apart, weight evenly spread.

● Concentrate — and be ready for anything.

● Catch with two hands if you can.

● Make sure you don't get in a tangle with other fielders — stay in your own territory.

Fielding Tips

1 If you're in an outfielding position and retrieving a ball from the boundary, DON'T run with the ball to reduce the distance you have to throw. Instead, throw the ball with a flat trajectory so it bounces In front of the 'keeper and bounces into his or her hands.

2 Always expect the ball to be hit to you. To help you concentrate when you are an out-fielder walk towards the batsman as the ball is being bowled.

3 Keep an eye on your captain and the bowler to catch any signal to adjust your position in the field.

4 DON'T get right underneath a high overhead catch — keep slightly away from the ball as it drops, adjusting your position in the last few yards.

5 If a ball goes up between two of you, DON'T get in a tangle — the first one to shout 'mine!' should go for it. Be decisive.

6 Close-in fielders should be stooped and ready for catches.

7 When returning the ball to the bowler do it gently and at an easily catchable height.

8 Don't forget to back-up the bowler or wicketkeeper to prevent any overthrow.

9 Don't wander about. Keep to the position your captain has indicated to you.

10 DO use both hands to stop a ball whenever possible.

11 On bright days wearing a cap is useful and helps avoid missing the ball when the sun is in your eyes.

Wicketkeeping

Many players rate wicketkeeping as the most exciting and challenging position of all. To be a good 'keeper, you'll need courage, quick footwork, a good eye, patience and safe hands. Plus, of course, plenty of practice!

Stance

Take up a relaxed stance behind the wicket, just far enough away to be able to remove the balls with an easy sweep (slow bowling).

● Squat down with knees fully bent: don't start to rise until the ball is on its way.

● Your hands should be together, with fingers pointing down just touching the ground behind the crease.

● Your heels need to be off the ground with your feet apart.

Taking the ball

● Find out what the bowler is doing and keep your eyes on the ball.

● Don't grab or snatch at the ball — get behind it and let it come to you.

● Watch the ball all the way into your hands.

● Run after a ball if you think you can save a run.

● Once you have the ball, turn your attention to the stumps — but watch the batsman's feet and don't remove the bails unless he's out of his ground.

● When taking a return from the field, always stay within reach of the stumps — speed in removing the bails is your top priority

Hint box: wicketkeeping

● Stand right up to the wicket or right back — never half-way.
● Watch the ball from the moment it leaves the bowler's hand until it is in your gloves or the batsman has hit it.
● Don't let the movement of the bat put you off — keep your eyes on the ball.
● Don't snatch at the ball — let your fingers 'ride' with it.

FITNESS AND PRACTICE

Fitness

Cricket is a physical game which requires a good all-round level of fitness. As with all sports it is important to keep in good shape and in top condition.

Warming up

This is an essential part of the game as it reduces the possibility of injury during the game. Start with a whole-body warm-up such as light running or skipping. Then continue with gentle stretching and loosening exercises, trying to use all the major muscle groups.

Practice

Because cricket is a team game, you should take every opportunity to practise with your team-mates, preferably with the help of a coach or more experienced player who can help correct any faults. But here are some additional suggestions for improving your game on your own.

Practise batting

Batting straight is most important. Get into playing a straight bat naturally, by practising forward and backward defensive strokes along a straight line. You may even be able to do this indoors using the line of a floorboard as a guide.

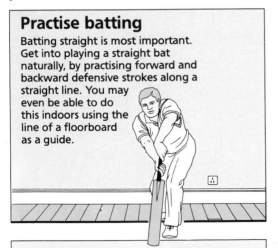

Tip: strengthen your grip for batting by hitting a soft ball repeatedly against a wall using your top hand only.

Practise throwing

Put an old tyre in a field and see how many times you can pitch the ball into it. Start 15yds (13.7m) away, then increase the distance to 20yds (18.2m), then 25yds (22.9m) and so on. Try to beat your own record next time or play in competition with a friend.

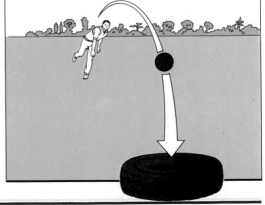

Watch television

You can learn a lot from watching the experts and their methods.

● See how the batsmen get into position and make their strokes.

● Watch carefully the slow-motion replays and listen to the commentary.

● See how the non-striking batsman backs up.

● Watch how the outfielders move in and the infielders concentrate as the bowler runs up.

Net practice

Net practice is an excellent way of improving your bowling and batting. Most clubs and schools are now equipped with nets. However, incorrect usage of the nets can encourage bad play; there's no point in repeating the same mistakes. So it's best to have a good coach on hand. Remember batsmen, it's also good practice for the bowlers!

Practise bowling

Mark out a pitch, put in the stumps and then place a handkerchief in front of the stumps on a good length. Now with your normal bowling action see how many times you can hit the handkerchief and the stumps with the same delivery. Try to beat your record next time, or play in competition with a friend.

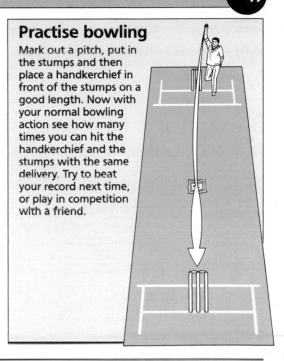

Glossary

This glossary explains terms found in the text, and some others you will encounter when watching or playing the game.

APPEAL   A call to the umpire by one of the fielding side to give a batsman out.

BLOCK   Mark made by the batsman to indicate his *guard* in front of the wicket.

BOWLING CREASE   The line on the pitch along which the stumps are positioned.

BREAK   The deviation of a ball from its straight path after hitting the pitch

BYE   A run made when the ball passes the wicket without being touched by the bat (cf *leg bye*).

CENTURY   An individual batting score of 100 runs.

CLOSE FIELD   The fielders close to the batsman (cf *deep*).

CUT   A stroke made at a short-pitched ball on the off side.

CREASES   Lines on the pitch — cf *bowling crease, popping crease, return crease.*

DEAD BALL   A ball that is out of play, eg at the end of an *over*, or when a batsman is out, or when it has finally settled in the hands of the bowler or wicketkeeper.

DECLARING   Except in senior *limited-over matches*, a batting side may at any time declare their innings closed, in order to try to produce a result rather than a *draw*.

DEEP — The fielders away from the pitch near to the boundary (cf *close field*).

DRIVE — A batting stroke made with a full downward swing of the bat.

DUCK — A score of nought (cf *golden duck*).

EXTRAS — Runs added to the score made without striking the ball with the bat. cf *bye*, *leg bye*, *wide* and *no-ball*.

FOLLOW-ON RULE — Rule by which the second team to bat in a two-innings match can be asked to bat again if they are losing by more than a specified number of runs.

FULL PITCH — A ball delivered that reaches the batsman without touching the ground first — also known as a *full toss*.

GLANCE — A ball deflected off the face of the bat.

GOLDEN DUCK — Being out for a golden duck means being dismissed with no score on your first ball.

GOOD LENGTH — A delivery which pitches at such a point as to cause maximum problems for the batsman.

GOOGLY — An off-break delivery made with a leg-spin bowling action.

GUARD — The batsman's preferred position in relation to the stumps. cf *block*.

HALF-VOLLEY — A delivery which pitches beyond a *good length*.

HAT TRICK — When a bowler gets three batsmen out with consecutive deliveries, not necessarily in the same over or even innings, but in the same match.

HOOK — A stroke made to the leg-side off the back foot at a short-pitched delivery.

INNINGS — A period of play during which a team takes its turn at batting.

IN-SWINGER — A delivery which moves from *off* to *leg side* while in the air.

LBW — Leg Before Wicket — a form of dismissal where the batsman intercepts a ball with any part of his body which would otherwise have hit the wicket.

LEG BYE — A run scored when the ball is deflected past the wicket unintentionally by the batsman, with anything other than the bat or hand holding the bat cf *bye*.

LEG SIDE — The side of the pitch on which the batsman stands to receive the ball. Also called *on side* (cf *off side*).

LENGTH — The point where the ball pitches after it has been bowled. (cf *good length*).

LIMITED-OVER MATCH — This is where the number of *overs* are agreed upon before the match starts.

MAIDEN OVER — An *over* in which the batsman fails to score any runs.

NO-BALL — If the umpire considers any delivery to be unfair, a 'no-ball' is called and an extra delivery added at the end of the over.

NOT OUT — If a batsman has not been dismissed at the end of an innings, he is said to be 'not out'.

OFF SIDE — The side of the pitch on which the batsman does not stand (cf *leg side*).

ON SIDE — See *leg side*.

OUTFIELD — The part of the field away from the pitch.

OUT-SWINGER — A delivery which moves from leg to off while in the air.

OVER — Six deliveries by one bowler constitute an over; overs are delivered from alternate ends of the pitch by different bowlers.

OVERTHROW — When a fielder throws the ball past the wicketkeeper allowing the batsmen to add more runs to their score.

POPPING CREASE — Line marked parallel to the *bowling crease* and in front of the wickets.

PULL — An attacking stroke which pulls the ball off the back foot.

RETURN CREASE — The line drawn at right angles to the *popping crease* and the *bowling crease*.

SQUARE CUT — A stroke made off the back foot to a short delivery just outside the off stump.

SWEEP — A batting stroke in which the ball is hit to the leg side with a sweeping movement and a horizontal bat.

WIDE — A ball is called 'Wide' if the umpire considers it too high or too wide of the stumps for the batsman to play.

YORKER — A delivery which pitches around the batsman's feet.